The Gremlin Theater presents

Outside Paducah

The Wars at Home

By J.A. Moad II

Premiered in Minnesota at the Bloomington Center for the Arts

10 November 2016

Supported in part by the Minnesota Humanities Center

ISBN 10: 0-9986477-0-5
ISBN 13: 978-0-9986477-0-8
War-Torn Books
Northfield, Minnesota

W T   WAR-Torn Books

Outside Paducah

By J.A. Moad II

Cast

The Boy, The Father & The Veteran | **J.A. Moad II**

Creative Team

Director | **Leah Cooper**
Technical Director/Design | **Carl Schoenborn**
Lighting | **Erin Belpedi**
Sound | **Katharine Horowitz**
Stage Manager | **Sarah Bauer**
Imagery | **Erin Belpedi & J.A. Moad II**
Costumes | **A. Emily Heaney**
Producer | **Peter Christian Hansen**

Praise for *Outside Paducah*

A brilliant portrayal of war's devastating reach beyond the battlefield. Line-by-trenchant-line and scene-by-evocative-scene, *Outside Paducah* precisely locates the gravitational pull of war in individual longing to fulfill family traditions and community histories that prove as treacherous as they are alluring.

Peter Molin – Time Out

His writing is deeply humane, creating characters that ring true and whose emotions seep into our consciousness, prompting tenderness toward these wounded guys, and dismay at the systems that inflicted their wounds. They reveal themselves not through sweeping statements, but through the large and small tribulations of getting through their days.

Arthur Dorman – Talkin' Broadway

I encourage readers to recite the work aloud; the aural landscape of this work is finely textured, and the characters come alive when given to the air.

Brian Turner – author of *Here Bullet*

Dedication

To my parents, who taught me to believe in the power of imagination, rendered with conviction and discipline. And to Michelle, Marcus and Audrey, who've endured living with a writer and an actor in denial. You gave me the love, support and space to write, create, grow and learn. Thank you.

Special acknowledgments to Leah Cooper, who believed in me, saw what I couldn't, and coaxed my inner actor into existence. Your wisdom and patience are a gift to us all.

And to Scott Allen, who pushed me to perform. As an original cast member of *A Chorus Line*, your certainty and inspiration helped me believe. I'll always cherish the quote you inscribed on the card you delivered to me:

> *You've got to know your limitations. I don't know what your limitations are. I found out what mine were when I was twelve. I found out that there weren't too many limitations if I did it my way.*
>
> Johnny Cash

And to all my wonderful friends and colleagues whose donations and support made it possible to bring this work to the stage.

David Abrams, John Battiste, David & Sarah Beimers, Tara Nesbit de Cardenas, Hosmer Brown, Gary and Mary Carlson, Stephen Clemens, Doug Cunningham, Stacey Engels, Michelle Loftus Flynn, Jesse Goolsby, Ross Gresham, Robert Goulburn, Mariana Grohowski, Rachael Hanel, Patrick Hicks, Nancy Kauffman, Neal Karlen, Chris King, Carson Kreitzer, Susan Jaret McKinstry, Pete Molin, Anne Knowler, Jennifer Kumble, Eric Lindamood, Betsy Marro, Tom and Angie Meagher, Trista Matascastillo, Hardy Montoya, Sarah Myers. David O'Fallon, Susannah Ottaway, Joe Pahr, Gloria Reading, Katey Schultz, Margret Swanson, Tanya Trout-Bainbridge, Cynthia VanRenterghem, Becky Warren, Jonathan Wei, Jennifer Will, Andria Williams, Christine & Joe Williams, Chante Wolf, and Phil Zrimsek

Outside Paducah

Part I – *Our Ghost*

All three parts of the play are solo performances. The first one has an adult man playing the part of a boy. A large projection screen should be used throughout the performance to show images and serve as background for all three parts of the play. Every part of the set should remain somewhere as a reminder of the stories rendered before. The reason will become apparent at the end of the play.

Characters

The Boy	A seven year-old boy from Mound City, IL.
Setting:	June, 2007. Early evening. A small house on the outskirts of Mound City. Upstage right, the back of a modest house with two large windows and a wooden porch that is noticeably burned on one corner. An empty rocking chair and a stuffed animal dog (Pesky) sit on the porch. The backseat bench of a car sits next to the porch. The sun is setting below the house.

(Photos of soldiers' faces with the thousand-yard stare populate the screen. They are from several wars, including the American Civil War. They play until an image of a boy hanging from the barrel of a tank appears. It fades and is replaced by an image of trees. The Boy enters upstage left, shoots his gun, and moves downstage center. He stops and shoots up above the audience, playing a game of some sorts in his mind. He stops and places the gun on his shoulder.)

THE BOY

Sometimes they go with ya... Booo! That's what my friend Bennie said when I told him we'd be movin' on soon. I didn't want to believe him, ya know, and that scared me more than anything, cuz I was hopin' we'd leave that old ghost behind.

(Motions toward the trees.)

Bennie's got an older sister, but ain't either of us got a brother, so we's about as close as close can be. He knows all about ghosts. They even watch a TV show about 'em. Invited me over once to watch once, but I ain't got no interest in seein' 'em TV since I got a real one of my own.

(Lowers gun to the ground.)

Bennie says that ghosts ain't got no sense of time, that they didn't make it over to the other side, and just keep movin' from one place in time to another. They's restless, he says, and if they catch you lookin' at 'em then they'll follow you. Sometimes they go back to when they died and watch it over and over again. That must be why it's so sad and angry all the time, but I put that notion away and didn't linger on it too long.

(Looks stage left.)

I was hopin' Bennie might play awhile longer, this bein' my last night and all, but his mama done called him home for supper.

(Plays with gun. Resigned.)

I guess it don't matter much since we's all played out anyway.

(Moves as if he sees Bennie, runs upstage left, waves and yells.)

I'll see ya!

(Glances at house, moves toward the porch a bit frightened. Reconnects with the audience.)

Last week the ghost did some awful screaming in the night. I heard mama talking it down, sayin' how it needed to "stop it right now." She asked God to step in and give her a hand, and I think that done the trick for a while.

(Looks at gun, pondering possibilities.)

I asked Bennie if he thought we could kill it with these here guns? He's almost eight, a full nine months and a day older than I am, and I thought he just might know. His daddy give him two bb guns for Christmas, and we use 'em to play war between their house and ours. There's a whole patch of trees there for hidin' behind. He said I could keep this here gun and take it with me, but my mama said noooo... Told me we ain't got no use for guns anymore... She took both of papa's rifles out of the house before he come back from the war. I thought he might put up a fight about it, but he don't say or do much about nothin' these days.

(Points toward porch.)

When it's nice out, mama sets papa out here in that old rocking chair facing us boys. He likes to stare out into the trees. I always straighten out his baseball cap before I go on and play. No matter how awful tired he is, it's nice to know he's watchin' over me.

Bennie says there ain't no need to kill the ghost cuz it's already dead. I guess he's right, but it sure sounds alive to me. He asked if I ever actual seen it, and the truth is, I ain't, and I hope I never do.

(Points gun above crowd and shoots. Next section rendered with pride and hope for dad to be strong.)

Bennie's a better shot than I am, but I wanna be a SNIPER some day, so I been practicin' to get a good eye. I know it's in me, cuz my papa was a sniper. Ain't sure what that means exactly, but I know he was good at shootin'... Sometimes I wish he would just kill that ghost and get it gone for good... A real gun might do the trick, but he's got the slowness now, and he ain't up for killin' much of anything these days. Mama said they's gonna make him all better up at the VA... give him all the medicine he needs. That's why we gotta go. I ain't scared or nothin', but it'd sure be nice if we could get things back to normal.

One time, I told Bennie about how my grandpa tried to kill the ghost, but he didn't say nothin'... He just looked away and that was about as far as we took the talk before we got back to killing each other and anything else we saw fit to shoot at.

> *(Rendered as if telling a secret. Points a pretend hand gun in the area of his head as if trying to shoot an imaginary ghost.)*

I heard all about it, though, how it got on Grandpa so bad one night that he took a shot at it—BANG... but he missed... Bullet went right through Grandpa's brain instead. Killed him dead. Mama don't say nothin' about it, since it was her daddy and all, but I know it's true.

> *(Looks at his gun, as if trying to shoot the ghost on him as he says the next line.)*

I sure hope the ghost never gets on me like that...

> *(Aims it at his head, touches trigger and moves gun away at the last second.)*

I guess my grandpa wadn't as good a shot as my papa.

(Lowers the weapon. Looks at his feet and then the trees. Aims the rifle above the audience.)

You know what Bennie says… he says there ain't nobody as good a shot as my daddy. And that always makes me smile.

(Glances toward house and then out toward the "land" in front of him.)

Mama says there's been a ghost on the land as long as she can recall. It comes and goes, and I knows she's right cuz she told me about the screamin' back when she was a girl. Sometimes at night, it puts off a horrible howlin' sound, and I hide under the blanket with Pesky. Pesky's my German shepherd.

(Points to Pesky on the porch.)

That's him… right there… He's not a real one, cuz they cost too much money to feed and all. He's stuffed, but he's as real as real can be, I got no doubt about that. One time he woke me up when papa left a cigarette burnin'. Caught the porch on fire. If it wadn't for Pesky, I bet this place mighta burned up like a torch. I seen a trailer down the road where that happened, and I felt bad for those folks. We been hopin' to get it fixed, but mama says we gotta wait for things to get better first.

(Sound of crickets. Slaps a mosquito on his cheek.)

Skeeters are startin' to bite…

(Walks toward the porch.)

Bennie' dad says the river's running high this year. Gonna be a whole mess of 'em this summer, so maybe it'll be good to be on our way.

(Look toward the house and points.)

That's my mama in the kitchen there... She's pretty. She's helping papa pack. These days she's always on the phone talkin' and waitin' to talk with folks up at the VA.

(Slaps his arm, looks at blood, grossed out and wipes hand on pants.)

I bet if you stayed out here all night, them skeeters'd suck the blood right out of you until there wadn't nothin' left. Bennie said his daddy went up to Alaska once, and that the skeeters up there are so big they can kill just about anything—that if you leave a horse out in the wild, a whole swarm of 'em will suck the life right out of it.

(Shivers uncomfortably.)

Just thinking about a big old horse being sucked down to the bone makes me tingly all over.

(Looks toward the house and then into woods.)

I know it's time to head on in, but I ain't ready just yet. I'm all packed up and ready, so there ain't no hurry.

(Sits down on the porch corner and looks around, as if reminiscing. Places his gun down beside him.)

When I was little, I'd sit out here on my daddy's lap He'd open him up a big old can of beer and say, (*In father's voice*) 'Hey son, how 'bout we linger out here awhile longer and listen to the crickets start their evenin' talk...' He liked it when some of that cool night air worked its way up from the Ohio River. I like that, too.

(Looks past the house and then back toward the trees. Expresses pride in the next lines.)

We're on the north side of the River—the winning side, just across the ways from Paducah. Sometimes when I play in these here woods, I think about how my family used to own all this land. I told Bennie about it once, but he said my head was full of rocks, and I didn't know nothin', but I know what Mama says, and she ain't never ever lied.

It was her great, great, great, great granddaddy that got it after the Civil War. Lt Joseph James was his name. Government gave him a hundred acres for fightin' in the War. He had a wooden leg, but he got on a horse anyways, and rode all the way out here from Pennsylvania. Musta been hard, ridin' all that way with a wooden leg and all, but I guess that's what heroes do. He's buried down the road in the big Civil War cemetery—A big old white tombstone with his name on it—LT JOSEPH JAMES. I seen it with my own two eyes... Mama says we's all that's left of him now.

There used to be a picture of him in his civil war uniform...

(Stands to side, rifle on shoulder, to show what the picture looked like.)

But it got lost back during the big flood. Must be sad to be some big War hero and have your picture get taken away by the river. It don't seem right somehow. I sure wish we still had it. We got lots of other pictures of war heroes in the family. There's my Grandpa, and my uncle Jake on my daddy's side, and then there's the one of my daddy right next to a big old American flag.

(Standing, gun to his side on the ground, to show what the picture looks like.)

He's one of them National Guard heroes that goes off when they come a callin'.

(Sets the gun against railing.)

He got into the fight twice. I don't remember the first time he went cuz I was just a kid and all, but I seen him off this last time... I didn't cry—not even once. He looked me right in the eye and said "there ain't no need for a big boy like you to cry..." and we shook hands on it. 'Course I missed him something awful—so awful that I didn't care what he was like when he come back at first... Ya see, he's got what folks 'round here call *the slowness*... Mama says the government's givin' him all the time he needs to get better, though. It'd sure be nice if they could give us some more land like they gave Lt James, but I guess they done give it all away.

(Steps forward, concern building.)

Bennie asked me if I thought the ghost might be Lt James... That maybe he's angry 'bout us losin' the land after he won it fair and square.

(Glances over shoulder then away.)

I guess maybe it could be, but I sure hope it ain't... Told him I'd ask my mama about it, and he said that whatever I do, don't look him in the eye. That if he sees you lookin' at him then he's bound to follow.

(Steps forward, shakes head.)

Can't see how the ghost would be angry at us, though. We ain't the ones who lost it all... Mama says her family kept splittin' the land in two when times got hard, selling it off bit by bit until they was down to an acre. We been doin' our best to hold onto it ever since. We ain't done nothin' wrong... nothing.

When mama told me the news... The first thing I did...

(Runs toward stage left.)

...Was go over and find Bennie in the trees. They got a real dog, an old mutt named Georgie, and they was out playin' fetch.

(Picks up an imaginary ball and throws it.)

Yep we's leavin' for sure, I said... Headin' up north to a special hospital just for snipers and other war heroes to get all better.

Georgie dropped the ball, but wadn't either of us in the mood to play

"Somebody gonna buy your place?" he asked.

(Shakes head and looks at the ground.)

Nope... with the ghost and all, folks been too scared to come around. The bank's gonna take it back.

(Steps away from Bennie.)

He didn't say it, but I know he's hopin' there'll be another boy movin' in, another boy to play with and go shootin' with... made me sorta sad to think I'd be replaced.

(Slides back to Bennie.)

"Think you'll ever be comin' back home," he asked, and I told him I didn't know one ways or another, but once papa gets all better, I couldn't see why not.

He liked the sound of that, and then he picked up the ball and let it loose on a long toss.

*(Takes a step back, looks into the distance as if
he can see the dog chasing it. Runs onto the
porch, picks up Pesky and gun, looks toward
them.)*

Someday I'm gonna get me a real dog, just like Georgie...

19

(Lights spotlight on him as he says goodbye to his gun. Leans it against railing.)

It's time now...

The car's all packed up and ready to go. I got Papa strapped in good and tight.

(Maturation and sense of responsibility.)

He ain't been drivin' since he come home cuz his arms don't work so well, but they's gonna fix him up real good. That's a fact... I heard that snipers are the most important people in the whole army! I guess being that important and all, he was used to gettin' driven around by folks.

(Steps off the porch.)

Bennie ain't outside cuz we's already said our goodbyes, but I know he's watchin'. We's best friends and all, so...

(Walks toward stage left as if looking at Bennie's house. Clutches Pesky to his chest.)

I bet he's lookin' out the window, thinkin' he might just see the ghost... I been trying not to, but that's all I been thinkin' about lately. I was gonna ask mama about it, but she's been on the phone all day, and I think she's done talked out.

(Yells toward house in brave tone.)

We're ready mama.

(Sits in the left side of the car and his eyes follow his mom as she leaves the house and walks to his car door. She closes it, and he watches her get in the front seat—Sound of both car doors closing.)

Don't you worry 'bout nothin', mama. Me and Pesky'll keep a watch over everything.

(Car starts. Glances at house, and then looks away quickly.)

It's real... we's actually goin'...

(Takes hold of his father's hand. Stifling his fear.)

I squeeze papa's hand, hopin' he'll squeeze back, but there ain't much there... He leans into the window lookin' hard as if he can see somethin' we can't... Don't look, daddy!

(Glances up toward his mom, trying to be strong.)

We'll leave that old ghost behind, mama!

I wanna believe it, but deep down I ain't so sure. Maybe Bennie's right. Maybe the ghost is Lt. James, after all, and he's out there looking for us, angry that we lost it all. There ain't nobody else to blame, but us... Maybe he's gonna follow us right up to the VA and won't let us be until we make things right.

(Looks into the rearview mirror.)

I can see mama's face in the mirror. She ain't cryin' like I thought she would. I guess maybe she's too scared to cry.

(His eyes follow his mother's movement.)

She reaches out toward papa and then her eyes settle on me. "Don't you look back, honey... Just... don't."

(Squeezes Pesky to his chest.)

I ain't gonna, mama... I ain't gonna.

(Sound of car driving away.)

(Lights fade.)

Part II – Cairo (pronounced K-Row)

Production Notes:

This is a discussion between a father trying to get a loan and a banker. The banker's questions are paraphrased by the Father aloud as if he's reflecting on them before answering (depicted in bold type). The questions seem basic at first, but the annoyance and frustration builds as the piece goes on. It is a struggle for the father to maintain his composure as he confronts the reality of everything that has happened to him. Throughout the piece, the Father's memories are rendered when he leaves the chair and steps into the spotlight. These thoughts are depicted in italics.

Characters

The Father
: A 51 year-old white man, originally from Southern Illinois, now residing in Ballard County, Kentucky, west of Paducah, across the river from Cairo, IL.

Setting:
: July, 2007. Outside a bank and also the interior of a bank manager's office on the west side of Paducah, Kentucky. A large window looks into the west, out over the Ohio River. A painting of Mount Rushmore is on the wall. Two empty formal wooden chairs sit just right of center stage.

(Photos of Cairo, Illinois, depicting racial strife and decay, followed by images of a devastated Iraq during the war. Once they've all been shown, the image of a bank building fills the screen. A man enters upstage left dressed in blue-collar attire. He wears a baseball hat with "Dan's Demolition" on it. He walks back and forth. Nervous.)

THE FATHER

You got this... just don' talk too much... You always talk too damn much. Just tell the man what he wants to hear and not another word.

(Takes business card from shirt pocket, reads it.)

Mr. Simms is his name. Likes a little face-to-face to see what a man's all about... Well... you show him. Folks say he appreciates a fine cigar. He'll offer you one if you're worth the risk.

(Returns card to pocket.)

He'll have heard the talk. No denyin' it, but you ain't got nothin' to confess.

*(Removes two objects wrapped in a handkerchief
from his pocket, unwraps and looks at them.)*

Just don't... go there. This is about what a man can do with his own two hands... Time to start believin' again.

*(Returns objects to pocket, walks to bank
entrance, slides hands down shirt, and steps into
the office.)*

Appreciate you meetin' with me, Mr. Simms.

*(Sits down and the image of the bank changes to
a picture of Mt. Rushmore. He motions toward it.)*

That's a fine picture of Mt. Rushmore ya got there. I been to the Black Hills once... Sure was somethin' special.

(Sits up, nods as if listening to the man's words.)

Yes sir, that's a fact. Paducah's a fine place... Been here goin' on ten years... Started Dan's Demolition back in '97. You see, that's why I'm here today, I was hopin' to—

(Stops after being interrupted.)

Yes sir, that's right... My daddy grew up in these parts. Ballard County, right across the river from Cairo. Graduated from Heath High School. Class of '42.

(Looks past Mr. Simms.)

In fact...

(Points toward the window, searching.)

If you look hard, you can see it. Right there where the Ohio River bends down toward Cairo. A clump of trees 'round a little pond... My daddy and his buddies would skip school and go fishin' there... did their best to let go of all the problems in the world back then... Three of 'em joined the Marines after high school. Shipped off to Guadalcanal together... My daddy was the only one to make it home. I asked him about it once, but he just said a man had to be there to know... Never said another word about it.

(Reaches out to the window. Nervous.)

That sure is a mighty fine view from here, Mr. Simms...

(Stands and steps into the spotlight.)

They're out there in the tool shed again... talkin' in their whiskey voices. Veterans' Day or Memorial Day... I get 'em confused. They carve names onto the wall and cry like little boys... What's wrong, dad? Tell me... please... We can make it all better... I promise.

(Returns to his seat.)

He was a carpenter, sir. Worked hard to build us a life up north near St. Louis. Talked about retirin' down here some day, but the good Lord took him home first... I fed him ice cream on the day he died—a chocolate, caramel swirl. The nurse said no, but I figured there ain't been a man yet who died from the taste of something sweet.

What kind of man was he?

(Happy at the interest in his dad. Enjoys telling this.)

The good kind. Not the church-goin' type, but the kind of man willin' to give a hand up to those in need. Said it gave him a purpose in life. Preferred talkin' to the Good Lord at a fishin' pond instead of church, so we'd spend our Sundays drivin' the back roads, past some school or bank he'd worked on after the war... He'd glide by and go on and on about the need for building things to last... He wadn't much of a fisherman, no sir, but he believed a man could do anything if given a chance.

(Steps into spotlight, slips to his knees, and draws a fourteen-inch screen in the air.)

1962. Our first T.V. A fourteen inch, black and white screen... And I can't take my eyes off it... Saturday morning cartoons... The Flintstones and the Jetsons. The President says we're going to the moon... the moon... I picture us all climbing into the car and driving there together. It all seems so possible...

You cloud over at the nightly news, dad. They've built a wall in Berlin, the President shot dead, more and more troops heading to Vietnam... You get lost in your work. [Stands] *I turn ten and you take me into city to see what you're building. I remember that day, dad... How you told me to close my eyes* [Closes eyes] *before we crossed the river, and I listened... You placed a hard hat on my head and when I looked up...* [Opens eyes] *It was right there in front of*

me... The Gateway Arch climbing into the sky like two arms comin'
together as one... It was beautiful. [Arms rise into an arch and then
he hugs himself.]

(Returns to his seat.)

I was hopin' to be like my daddy, Mr. Simms... Tried my hand at
buildin' a clubhouse, but I couldn't get it right, so I'd rip it down
instead. And, well... that was the fun part, I found myself buildin'
things up just to tear 'em down... Never thought about it before,
but maybe that's how I got interested in the business.

Yes, sir. That's right. I decided to give the Army a try.

Wanted to serve like my old man. He was strugglin' to make sense
of the times back then. Men givin' up and running off to Canada—
soldiers throwin' their medals away... Broke my daddy's heart to
see it... Said those men lost hope in this big country—forgot what
the fight was all about—freedom for all those folks over there.

(Steps back into the spotlight. Draws a larger TV
screen. Excited.)

A giant, brand new, big screen TV... 23 Inches... It's all there in
color... Everything... everything... Soldiers bleeding in the jungle,
helicopters and body bags... The burning skies... You don't watch
with me anymore, dad... People marchin' in the streets, police dogs
and assassinations... I wonder if we'll ever get to the moon.

(Returns to his seat.)

No sir, I never made it over to Vietnam.

...But I seen the troops come home... Folks say it was the war that
broke those soldiers, Mr. Simms, but it was more than that... Our
troops were over there fightin' to survive, just struggling to get
from one day to the next, and the truth is, we didn't wanna win
that war, and they knew it... I think down deep, we all knew it...

29

Ya see, a soldier has to believe we're all in the fight together. Take that away, and it can eat at a man—hollow 'em out 'til they're just a shell on the inside... It ain't what folks wanna hear, no sir, but the fact is, we gave up on those men... That's why so many of 'em ended up on the streets... why so many of 'em... Well... I did my time and got out... An honorable discharge... I missed my war.

(Rubs hands, uncomfortable. Frustrated at the interrogation.)

How'd I end up outside... Paducah?

(Deep breath, sigh. Defensive.)

When a woman runs off and leaves you to raise your son on your own, well... it tests a man. It's easy to lose your way... easy to get lost in a bottle and forget it's all about that little freckle-faced boy lookin' up at you with those scared eyes filled with questions... And the sad truth is, you ain't got an answer, no sir, cuz there ain't an answer in this whole damn world that makes sense.

I had a cousin down in Ballard County—a dry county. Said he could use a strong pair of hands, and I figured a dry county would do me good... Packed it all up and headed south. Told my boy we was goin' home.

(Exhales. Trying to focus and get back on track.)

Started Dan's Demolition a year later...

(Points to his hat—proud.)

And I worked hard—real hard, and folks 'round here took notice.

(Mr. Simms takes out a cigar.)

No sir, I don't mind the smell of a good cigar. You go right ahead.

(Aside) *He'll offer you one... Just...*

So, what drew a man like me to Cairo?

...It was my son, sir. He was struggling at the middle school. Couldn't buy a friend. Always in trouble for drawin' pictures in class, and then there was that shootin' over at Heath High School... Remember that? Some kid firin' into a prayer circle and killin' those three girls... They say he just stood there after he done it, dropped his gun and told the principle to shoot him... strange, huh, planned it out step by step, but it wadn't real until he saw the bodies.

(Uncomfortable reflective pause.)

I don't remember that kid's name, but I remember what they were calling him on the TV down here... a fourteen year-old gun-man. Not *boy with a gun*, but gun-man, as if killin' was all it took to make a boy into a man... Now I'm all about the right to a weapon, but my son was all I had in the world... No parent ever expects to lose their child, Mr. Simms... I figured there had to be another way. Thought we'd give home-schooling a try...

Heard about a librarian across the river in Cairo—an old Irish woman workin' magic with boys like him, so I set up a meetin'... Ester was her name. My son brought his drawings with him, a big old stack of 'em, and she sat right down and had a look-see at every one. Gave me a little wink, and when she ran her fingers through that red hair of his, it was like that boy come alive again... Two years... We'd been down here almost two years, Mr. Simms... and that was the first time I seen him smile.

(Pausing, Realizing that Mr. Simms doesn't care.)

(Aside) *You know what he wants to hear. Just get on with it.*

(Matter of fact. Containing himself.)

I'd cross that bridge into Cairo five days a week, sir, every mornin' and afternoon, and after awhile you can't help but notice that lost look in a man's eye when you pass him by—the cracked sidewalks and broken windows. Now I've seen those looks before—seen 'em up close and personal. Now, I ain't ever been in combat, no sir, but I know how the war rages on inside a man. The Government don't give a Purple Heart for the wounds of the mind, Mr. Simms, but maybe they should... I know what it means to lose hope, sir, and the sad truth is, there ain't enough hope left in Cairo to fill a thimble.

(Resignation at having to impart what the banker knows. He thinks, this is NOT a confession.)

I did my best, sir, but when a man boxes up a need, well it tends to come out sideways. You find yourself over there at the liquor store more than you should, and when a beautiful woman asks if there's anything special she can do for you... well, the color of her skin don't matter much... Bell was her name... I couldn't take my eyes off her...

(Steps into the spotlight.)

Yes mam, I'm in town a lot these days... ya see, my boy's over at the library, he's... Those sure are some pretty eyes you got there, miss... You mind if I buy you a cup of coffee sometime... You don't do coffee... How 'bout I treat you to lunch, then... you don't do lunch, either... Well, what do you do... Oh... OH... well I ain't ever done anything like that, m'am... I mean... Bell... okay... (Looks at Bell in a different location) *Is that your real name, Bell? Or is that your working name? ...* (Aware he's offended her) *I'm sorry, I didn't mean to... I'll see you next Wednesday...*

(Returns to the chair.)

Me and her had a standing appointment. Once a week before I picked up my boy... That's all.

No sir, He didn't know... I never said a word about it.

(A happy reflective smile.)

Ya see, he was thrivin'—Math, art, writin'... you name it... Old Ester workin' her magic... had him drawin' pictures of all the old buildings in town. Said it helped him make sense of the history there, and once he got behind the wheel there wadn't no stopping him, no sir. He'd glide through town and go on and on about Cairo bein' the tip of the spear in the Civil War, 'bout how those old slaves built it into something' special: mansions and music halls... the cobblestone streets... prosperous times back before The Klan come to town—before the white folks gave up and run off... It's funny what a boy can teach you...

(Steps into the light. Speaking to his son.)

These are good, son—you got real talent... I like that one the most: The Gem Theater. We had one like that in our town when I was a boy... Now you keep at it, okay... You got somethin' special there... Don't let anyone EVER tell you any different.

(Returns to the chair.)

And yet we stopped going there... yes sir... Why?

(Stops as if forcing himself to remember.)

I found myself driving across the river one night... the whiskey talkin' to me. You wanna ask the girl to stop ... doin what she's doin' ... though you know she ain't got a choice. When Bell saw the empty bottle, she grabbed me by the hand and took me home with her... Said she didn't want me to die on the road.

And kindness like that... well... I started helpin' with the rent. No promises, just clean sheets and a little quiet conversation... once and awhile she'd open a bottle of wine and go on about needin' to believe in a better life out there—the world bending toward justice...talk of seeing what this big country has to offer, but bein' afraid of what she'd find out there.

(A sense of urgency/despair.)

(Aside) *Why? ...He wants to know why...*

We had a nice run, Bell and me, but one day I found my boy... standin' outside her door. He looked me in the eye, thinkin' maybe I'd have something to say, but I didn't... We just drove back across the river, instead... Never said another word about it... We just stopped goin' there...

(Pauses as the realization settles over him.)

Maybe that's the answer, Mr. Simms... that it's just easier not to go there anymore—easier not question the things you been hearin' your whole life. Ya see, I'd been goin' to Cairo for years, but the truth is, I never saw the possibilities there, no sir... but my boy... well... He'd seen it all up close—the cracked sidewalks and all... He saw things I couldn't.

(Looks at the back of his hands as emotion builds.)

I thought I was doing the right thing, Mr. Simms... tryin' to make Ballard County his home—our home, but I was wrong... Cairo was his home, sir. I just couldn't see it...

(Fights to control his frustration at next question.)

Yes sir, that's right. He decided to join the Marines.

It was those damn burning towers... he watched it over and over again. Couldn't take his eyes off it, and then one day he sat down and started drawing it all out on paper. I woke up one morning to find him holding an old picture of my daddy in his uniform, and that was that... They trained him as a combat medic, part of the first wave into Baghdad and what he saw there changed him—no denying it, but he was a believer. Volunteered for a second tour, hopin' to finish what they started.

Said the hardest part was fightin' a battle they wadn't ready for. Folks killing each other for no reason... He got a little shrapnel in his leg and lost a buddy, but that ain't what did it, no sir. It was what folks started sayin' when he got back... that it wadn't worth the price... (*shakes head*) It never makes sense, does it...? One minute it's all about freedom and the next it's all just a big mistake...

(Trying to find the positive.)

After he got out I put him to work for me right away. He was strugglin', searchin' for a sense of purpose again, and when they offered us that demo job in Cairo, he got excited about the possibilities... I sent him there to scout it out—two old buildings rottin' on the inside... and well... all these years in the business, when you bring somethin' down it's cuz somethin' better's goin' up... Turns out there wadn't no plan to build.

(Aside) *Is that enough? ...How much does a man have to bleed before you give him a chance?*

The last time I was there?

(Resigned at the absurdity of another question.)

Ester's funeral. Whole town showed up... I looked for Bell, but word was she'd taken off with a truck driver... It ain't what folks wanna hear, but I don't regret my time there... The truth is, there wadn't much difference between Bell and me, just two folks stugglin' to get from one day to the next... I don't care what anyone says, Mr. Simms, I like to think me and her had somethin' special for awhile...

(Angry at himself for not being aware of how truly special it was. The emotion pushes him to stand and turn away. Regains composure and stands behind the chair.)

It's been a hard year, sir... days when I wake up a little lost and I find myself driving back across the river. Sometimes I park outside the library and try to get inside my son's mind.

(Light changes to reflect the memory expressed.)

I close my eyes and imagine us all there together—the city alive and thrivin', the Gem Theater and the music halls lightin' up the night, Bell and me steppin' out on the town... She's in a long red dress, walkin' tall in high heels. I lean into her and promise we'll hit the road together—see everything this big country has to offer... from the Black Hills to the desert sky... I swear, if she ever comes back, I'll make good on my word.

(Hesitant and then defiant.)

It ain't right...

(Shaking his head. Revelation.)

I know what folks 'round here been sayin'... that I did it to myself, that we shouldn't have gone there. The same old stories about how the black folks killed that place... Except they say it in their own SPECIAL way down here—don't they, Mr. Simms... But they're wrong. The folks there just lost hope. WE gave up on 'em... I don't care what anyone says, Cairo didn't die cuz of poor black folks. Cairo died from a broken heart.

(Pauses, aware he's said too much.)

(A hard aside) *Don't put out your cigar... I ain't askin' for much.*

36

*(Sits back down. Contrite. The need for approval
taking over.)*

We all got a war in our past, Mr. Simms, and it changes you. If a man wants to rebuild a life, he has to accept the changes. I see that now... I seen it up close and personal. I've learned what it means to walk the streets alone—to step down those cracked sidewalks and look in through a broken window at a life you can't get back... When you see your son's body hanging from the rafters of a building a man has a choice to make. When you hold him in your arms, you ask yourself if you're worthy of the life you've been given, and when you close his eyes for good, you either start believing again or else you'll get trapped right there forever.

(A hard aside) Don't look away from me... I am worth the risk.

(Fighting to keep his frustration in check.)

I've made mistakes, sir... done things I ain't proud of, but that don't mean I've stopped trustin' in what I can do with my own two hands.

*(Pulls out handkerchief, unfolds objects, and
places one in each hand. Opens his palms for Mr.
Simms to see. Certainty in his voice here.)*

I want to show you something, Mr. Simms... This here's my daddy's Purple Heart, and this here's my son's, and each and every morning I wake up searchin' for a way to be worthy of them... They're all I have left in the world.

(Offers them to Mr. Simms.)

Now you take these and hold onto 'em until I pay you back.

And you keep 'em safe, sir... please... Cuz I'll be payin' it all back... on time and with interest... That's a promise!

37

(Aware that Mr. Simms isn't going to take them. Steps around the desk and extends palms toward him.)

I'm asking you, sir... Can you help a man rebuild a life?

(Waits for him to answer. Keeps looking at him.)

Can you?

(Lights Fade.)

Part III – *Quittin' Meth*

<u>Production Notes:</u>

A former soldier is returning to his hometown for no particular reason. Staging and movement based on the specific set. Ideally a park bench is stage right and a bar is stage left. The fourth wall is broken from the first line on.

<u>Characters</u>

The Veteran   A 28 year-old white man, originally from Granite City, IL, now residing in the middle of Missouri. Dressed in jeans, combat boots and a baseball hat placed backwards on his head.

Setting: August, 2007. Granite City, IL, a rundown steel town. Outside and inside Sketcher Club, as well as the downtown residential area nearby, and a park bench across the street from his childhood home.

(A series of questions are projected on the wall, one at a time. These are the ones we should ask every person before they join the armed forces. Examples: http://wlajournal.com/blog/?p=713 An image of Sketchers Club populates the screen. The Veteran sits at the park bench, head down. Looks up and addresses audience.)

Are you ready for this? ...I hope so, because I sure as hell wasn't...
OR [*depending on audience response*] REALLY? Well, good for you,
because I sure as hell wasn't...

(Steps to center stage.)

I don't usually go to a joint like this. Ever. And by ever, I mean,
this new *ever* that I've been in for a while. But the thing is, a guy
forgets. Ya see, it's easy to forget because this isn't the kind of
place anyone plans to get lost in, that one-in-the-morning-still-
going-strong-place, where Pabst is the master of the house—a
fucking king who shapes the remnant of the night into whatever
you swore you'd never do again.

But you go there anyway.

(Motions toward the bar.)

You go there because sometimes you have to taste it all over
again. You have to feel the bite just to know it's real. And here at
Sketcher's, it's easy to get lost inside the tall cans of Red Bull,
Guinness, and shots of whiskey waiting to punch a hole in the
night.

(Steps in front of the park bench.)

Another short notice visit to see the old place. I gave Ike, Donny,
and Rich a call, but sometimes I don't tell a soul. I just hop onto
Highway 70 and head east, the sun setting behind me as the
Gateway Arch climbs into the sky glowing all orange and rusty
red. I cross the bridge into Illinois, and before I know it, I'm back
in the old downtown where I walk the streets alone.

*(Moves center stage and motions toward things
he describes them. Soft reminiscence.)*

42

And I can see what's long gone now, the park bench across the street, those monkey bars, swing sets and dirt fields where I played ball deep into dusk. My little sister and me racing on our bikes toward that spinning ice cream cone, and Betty's hair salon where my mother worked weekends.

(Rendered with bitterness that grows.)

And then I fall into the now—buildings for rent, cheap, real cheap—scary fucking cheap. The old Sears building has been sittin' empty for over a decade now, and the post office found a new strip mall to call home, but Sketchers… well Sketchers is goin' stronger than ever along with old Schmidt mortuary down the block.

(Two steps back as if falling into the town.)

And this town is everywhere and nowhere, A remnant of a place, strangely ordinary in its decay—an Econo Lodge-Dairy Queen-Dollar Store lovefest—a god-damned, chained-up nightmare, and it starts to eat at me, and more than ever I feel the weight and the pull of the street as if it's trying to take me back—trying to swallow me whole.

(Aware of his own bad choice.)

I should have known better when my best old buddy, Ike, stopped in at at 7-Eleven for some smokes. Ike's a realtor who hates people, and that's what I like about him. "One guy's dream house is another guy's nightmare," he likes to say. "And once you realize that, you own the world." He gets a kick out of selling some shit house or condo to some idiot who thinks he can flip it. "We're all just using each other, man…" and fuck if he ain't right.

(Steps forward taking the cigarette.)

He opens a pack of Camels and palms a cigarette into my hand. And you think by now I'd know better... That I'd be heading home instead of taking my first drag in nearly a year.

(Takes a long drag on the cigarette-relief.)

Midnight and I don't say no... Midnight and I've fucking signed up for the night and everything it has to offer, the two of us nodding in sync... Game on.

(Nodding as he flicks cigarette to the side. Moves stage left as he speaks next lines.)

Another cigarette, and I ride the wave of that long good burn back into town, past the pawnshop and rows of chain link fences... the old streetlights reminding me of what I've almost forgotten... And then I start to feel it again—that thing waking back up inside me, the thing I thought I'd killed off, but hadn't—the thing waiting there to take over when my defenses are down... And right now they're way down low—bent-over-pants-around-my-ankles-low... And I can see... though I don't want to see, my little sister in the back of my mind, her body bleeding a life away onto the pavement—those young eyes turning the world cold.

(Lingers on her image, and then angles back to the center as if the sound of the car door pulls him from the memory.)

And when the car door squeaks open into the wet-cool night, it hits me right away, that thick, burning-tire, sulfur smell in the air from what's left of the steel mill, the taste of it clinging to the back of my throat. I'm eight blocks away from where I grew up, the gravel twisting beneath my boot as we step toward the bar.

(Steps toward the bar and stops, the memory taking him out of the present. Looks above the audience, recalling.)

I can almost hear my old man telling me it's okay to walk down to Hit and Run and get him some smokes, even though...

(Slips into the memory.)

It's ten at night, and I'm only eleven, and we'd sat there watching the scary movies together—watched arms and legs chopped off by chainsaws, girls getting knifed in the shower, and Freddie Krueger finding his way into my dreams. I don't want to go—the fear my old man can see in my eyes, but he just laughs and says it isn't real...

(Steps from the memory.)

But for a kid, real has nothing to do with it.

(Looks at bar – Expresses joy. Stops.)

Outside Sketcher's, I hesitate, and for a moment I'm lost inside a haze of beautiful possibilities—ancient possibilities. I hear the music and picture all the empty hours drinking and imagining the days ahead... all of us dancing, and the laughter flowing from our mouths like wine...

But open the door now, and the story changes...

(Steps into the bar. Music and bar noise.)

There's nothing pretty about this place, with its second or third-hand feel, and just enough bad lighting to hide the acne scars and cheap mascara. Fifty drunks packed into a place meant to hold forty. Torn jeans and old combat boots, tramp stamps, and those pierced tongues that used to do it for me.

(Vulnerable. Directly to audience as if wanting to be understood.)

But that was just a phase, a short one I got lost in for awhile. Ya see life's like that for me—phases... Rooms we have in the mansions of our minds. I read that somewhere: *mansions of your mind.* A phrase like that can almost make you believe in things again if you let it... I'd like to think that inside of each of us there's a mansion, but the truth is, I think of it as a morgue instead— rooms of dead places, and faces that are long gone—nothing worth looking back at.

(Steps out of bar moves down center with a degree of swagger. Addresses the audience— confessional.)

So here's the shit: I've done bad things. Bad things were my job, and when you do your job right, the bad things rack up into a giant bill, and the only way to pay it off is to harvest the bad all over again, to get down and taste it, bite into the apple and smile while you're doing it... Ya see, it's all about normalizing the thing. It's a fucking détente with the beast within. The shrinks tell you it won't work, but they don't know—don't understand that you can't fill a burned out crater with flowers. They just rot and die. But the bad... ohhh, let me tell you, man, only bad can balance bad on the scale. It can keep you walking tall and strong—strong enough to choke the beast when it tries to swallow you whole...

(Angles toward bench. Stands beside it.)

I almost worked up the nerve to walk past my parent's old house today—my house for the first eighteen years of my life, but I couldn't. Ya see, it's really the burned out remnant of a house nobody cares to rebuild. The last renters had a meth lab in the basement. Boom. Shit happens. I heard about it from Ike, his email tunneling through to me on the other side of the world in Iraq... I don't know why, but all I could think about was that Tom Waits song, you know, the one where a guy lights his house on fire and sits across the street watching it burn all *Halloween orange and chimney red.*

*(Disconcerting thought—as if it doesn't quite
make sense. Sits on bench.)*

Even though my old man was already dead by then, I kept picturing him sitting across the street at that park bench watching it all go up in flames. And when I closed my eyes, I swear I could see the whole place burning all the way from that Baghdad morgue. It was as real to me as the stacks of bodies I was guarding from the eyes of the world. I'd seen enough shit burn by then... I'd seen it all, man—I'd...

*(Pauses as if uncertain about going on.
Confessional... Stands and moves center. Angry.)*

I'd peeked inside body bags filled with school kids and old women... That's right... I studied the open eyes of tortured men, their fingers and hands sliced away on the road to paradise. I'd seen the whole fucking world burn by then... I knew the color and smell of a long good burn... There wasn't anything GOOD about it.

(Steps back in the bar. Folsom Prison Blues plays.)

But right now, I don't care, cuz a fresh beer just found me, and there's a song spilling out of the jukebox like an old friend. (singing along) *Folsom Prison Blues...* God Damn, Johnny Cash... Fuck, how I love Johnny Cash. Reminds me of my old man—the good parts of him—the parts I choose to remember.

(Scans the room.)

And everyone's lost in the moment, humming along and mumbling the words cuz we know Johnny's right here with us, playing to his favorite crowd. We're all at one with the Man in Black...

(Watches the waitress serve them.)

Shots of Wild Turkey from the girl behind the bar, Trista, who slaps 'em down with a smile at Ike.

Another round and I start looking for somebody—a face to ground me—some guy from high school, a relative or some chick I've boned before, but I don't recognize a soul. Outside of a few spoiled college bitches and a handful of used cougars looking for some backseat action, there's nothing to tempt me. A good thing, I tell myself—a damn good thing.

(Glances over his shoulder.)

Donny and Rich are long gone. A steak and two beers before they beat feet back home to their wives in time for SportsCenter. They gave me that slap-on-the-back, *thanks for your service*-bullshit, that hits you like a hand job from your grandma. And then they picked up the check—the least they could do... Weak-dicks. I'm in town one fucking night, and they can't step it up a notch... But what do I expect, a parade? I never wanted that goddamn parade of lies.

None of us did.

(Steps outside the bar.)

The guys who wanted parades were the fucks who sent us over there for whatever fill-in-the-blank reason they wanted it to be... The Colonel said it was about *(Colonel's voice) the Vietnam Vets as much as us,* you know, *the guys who never had their chance, and how we should keep that in mind...*

And I tried.

(Sincere. Walks to the center.)

I really... really tried... but it was crazy surreal... I mean they gave us these new Humvees to ride in—Humvees that hadn't burned in the desert sun or felt the gritty sting of dust and sand in their engines. And it was this eerie, slow, stop and go. I'm talkin' lawn chairs and lemonade stands, people in sunglasses lining the roads to watch. And the whole time, it was like riding on the back of an invisible serpent, this giant thing slithering through the streets...

(Steps back as if observing—slows down.)

Little kids waving flags, women in tears, and the old combat vets in baseball hats—hands over their hearts... The guys I thought could see it, but I guess to see it, you have to want to see it.

(Desire to escape the memory. Back to the bar.)

Trista winks at me and drops a shot of Jaeger into a pint of Guinness. Kaboom. ...And then I see him, or at least what's left of him. I slide down the bar, and yeah, it's Will, his right leg replaced by something stuffed into an old tennis shoe.

(Slides down the bar.)

I saddle up beside him, and he looks up at me through these thin razor sharp eyes... Four years together playing football, but all I can see now is the dark hole of him, the way his mouth tucks into himself as if being swallowed by something inside. "Fallujah," he says, motioning toward his leg.

Enough said.

More drinks and more shit about the real shit, and he talks on and on, though I'm not askin' to know anything specific. Hints of what we know, but don't talk about—the burning skies, charcoal bodies, and the slick stain of death beneath our wheels as we rolled on and on... He keeps rubbing his hands together between small talk about his days at Walter Reed, the cocktails of drugs doled out like candy, and how he got lost inside it all.

(Looks away, semi-annoyed.)

I look away, but he won't shut the fuck up, and I don't know which story is which anymore, or what's real and isn't, everything coming together into a single heartbeat... And somewhere inside it all is a strange apology to me and the whole damn world, as if anyone could forgive anyone for what we'd seen and done.

(Looks into the distance... raises his glass.)

The music stops, and we raise our drinks. They say our soldiers are coming home for good... No more boots on the ground in Iraq... It's finished... really...?

(Builds to anger.)

No more sandstorms or bodies to retrieve from the alleys and rivers, no more looks from the people who want you gone or dead, no more roadside bombs or...

(Steps outside the bar. Bar music replaced by sound of confusion.)

And then everything begins to slow down, and I get that pit in the stomach, sinking sensation that a bomb is about to go off or— BOOM! And the whole place explodes inside my mind. The broken windows and body parts—the blood everywhere... This isn't real! The dead scattered all around me—people screaming... it's all in your mind...

(Frozen as if paralyzed by memory.)

I said it's not fucking real!

(Coming out of the memory.)

I scan the room and study everyone because I can't... help myself... it's all too real... it's nothing... Nothing... just a bunch of drunks, me included.

I stare at the door, and I want the music to take me... I want to sing along to the songs we once knew by heart, songs telling us what life was supposed to be like—songs that got it all wrong. I check out the girls who've just stumbled in. Eighteen or nineteen at best, eye-candy, and higher than a kite. A fake redhead glances my way, and I can feel that thing inside me clawing to get out... she just might do the trick, an apple ready to bite...

(Moves toward the girls. Stops. Notices Will.)

And then Will turns in his bar stool and looks the girls over. He licks his lips, and then spins back to his beer.

I try to smile, but I've got nothing left to add, no story to complete the night, and that's when Will reaches out to me for the first time. I can see the pockmarked hands now, and his wrist... scarred from a blade.

(Study's Will's wrists.)

It's just the two of us, no one else who can see what's right here with us. He puts his hand on the bar and looks through me... says he knew he'd reached the bottom when the only place left to fall was in a grave.

(Moves into Will's space and speaks in Will's voice.)

And you know how I came to quit it...Really knew, I mean, really fuckin' knew the fuckin' shit had taken me down... It was when the taste of fifteen year-old pussy wadn't cuttin' it anymore. When I started lookin' at my little sister's friends and thought maybe, just maybe that twelve-year old bitch could do it for me... You know how it is, man, right, right...?

(Nods and moves away as he speaks.)

And I nod... not knowing, yet knowing I always will.

No more words, just a last drink and our goodbyes lost somewhere between the empty dreams, music and nightmares. I slap a wad of bills on the bar and slip by the redhead, and then past Ike and Trista as if I'm a ghost they can't see...

(Exits bar and moves down center. Speaks to the audience. Image of steel mill appears on screen.)

Sometimes the bad doesn't have to be yours. It doesn't have to bite you. You ride the wave of it out into streets and feel the weight on your back—that thing you bear into forever, a poison tongue hissing its warning... You brush against the skin of it, and then you know.

(Moves down left as he speaks, stops and looks toward the house down stage right.)

Outside, a cool mist clings to the night and I find myself going back there, one step after another down the wet sidewalk. They said a handful of kids burned up in that basement—teenagers turned into torches, and I have to know that place again.

(Moves down right as he speaks.)

So I walk on past *Hit and Run* and the old post office, past the rows of chain link fences... I want to find it again, linger there and close my eyes. I want to hear my mom's voice, back when she used to sing and dance in the kitchen. I want to hear my sister scream when the car hits her, my old man pounding his fist against the wall until it gave in... I need to remember how we all surrendered to the anger and fear until it tore us apart and turned that house into something it wasn't meant to be.

(Moves back stage left as he speaks the next lines, then moves faster circling back toward the bench.)

The rain begins to fall, and I quicken my pace, faster and faster down the empty streets as if the whole world is chasing me. I turn down an alley, slip and fall. On and on I run until I turn the corner and stop—my hands and knees bleeding as I train my eyes on the park bench, trash, and weeds.

And here on the perimeter, I feel the weight of all those eyes—the lost, the dying and the dead, their silent screams reminding me of what we've all forgotten.

(Scans the set and slides onto the park bench.)

We're all here together now, and I reach out toward that place...

(Reaches out toward the audience.)

I want to go back.

(Pain and frustration building.)

I want to torch the night with light and set the sky on fire. I want to linger here and watch it spread. I want the world to see us burn all Halloween orange and chimney red.

(Stands defiant against the reality of everything.)

I want it all... to be beautiful again.

(Blackout.)

End of Play